RELATIONSHIP RESIDUE

BY
Cinse Bonino

see
choose
see

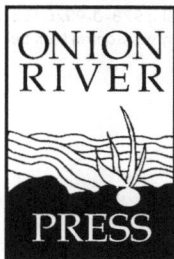

ONION
RIVER
PRESS

191 Bank Street
Burlington Vermont 05401

Also by Cinse Bonino:
The Ride of Your Life: choosing what drives you

ISBN: 978-0-9976458-9-7
Library of Congress Control Number: 2018939187

for Daddio

CONTENTS

CHAPTER 1
Leftovers

When you step in dog poop, it gets stuck on the sole of your shoe. This is a fact of life. You can wipe your shoes in the grass; you can scrape them over the edge of a step or a curb; you can even use a stick, but some of that steamy little doggie pile will undoubtedly and stubbornly adhere to the bottom of your shoe. Crappy experiences that happen in relationships can leave us with this same type of sticky ick.

When something profound happens to us in a relationship, especially when it is something negative we don't completely understand, it can continue to bother us long after the relationship is over. Often what sticks with us most are the negative emotions – fear, distrust, guilt, blame, hopelessness, or resentment – that arise from our unanswered questions: *Why did they do that? Don't they love me? What's wrong with me? What's wrong with them? Is this going to happen again? Is this always going to happen? How do I change this? Oh God, what if I can't do anything about this?*

These negative, lingering, leftover feelings invite us to do two things:

1. To believe all our relationships will be, or at the very least, have the potential to be, just like the one in which these negative things happened

2. To focus the majority of our energy on
scrutinizing our relationship in order to avoid
anything that would encourage these negative
things to happen to us again

These all-consuming posttraumatic concerns
repeatedly remind us of the awful things that have
happened to us. They also invite us to become
hyper-vigilant about protecting ourselves. We
may start to automatically mistrust the actions and
intentions of those who say they love us. With our
energy and focus wrapped up in these behaviors,
we may end up putting very little effort into creating
the kind of relationship we actually do want to have.

It doesn't matter what kind of relationship we
were in – familial, romantic, friendly, work-related,
traditional, or nontraditional. It doesn't matter who
wounded us – those responsible for us when we
were children, siblings, other relatives, our children,
friends, romantic partners, colleagues, or bosses. It
doesn't matter what age we were or are. It doesn't
matter what our gender, sex, or sexual preference is.
It doesn't matter what shape, color, or size of body
we have. All that matters, is that we are a human
being who has suffered some kind of substantial-to-
us pain – real or imagined, intended or accidental,
physical or emotional, large or small – at the hands

of another human being with whom we were in a relationship.

And much like the dog poop clinging to the bottom of our shoe, the residue that clings to us from bad relationship experiences can come along for the ride without our conscious knowledge. We may not notice it until we notice we have unintentionally carried it into our current relationship, just as when we are surprised to discover we have tracked dog poop onto our kitchen floor, even though we cleaned off our shoe after stepping in it.

Most of the examples used in this book are from romantic relationships; however, the issues and behaviors described can be present in any type of relationship. These descriptions are designed to help you notice not only what is happening in your relationship, but also why it may be happening. The behavioral approaches suggested are offered as opportunities for you to bravely increase your ability to make the kinds of choices that will help you to learn more about yourself. This self-knowledge will enable you to fine-tune your bullshit detector, whether you are pointing it at yourself or at others.

Remember: It's what you choose to do with your leftovers that matters.

CHAPTER 2
Role Play

What role does the other person in your relationship expect you to play? Are their expectations out-in-the-open or are they implied? How are these expectations communicated to you? Do you receive verbal or nonverbal approval when you behave in particular ways? Is disapproval expressed when you don't do what is expected of you? Does your partner ever withhold affection or distance themselves from you to punish you when you don't do what is expected? What do you expect from your partner? How do you convey *your* expectations?

Uncovering the intricacies of *expected* behaviors in a relationship can be difficult. It all starts with how specific roles were *imprinted* on us when we were young. We watched the people in our lives fill particular roles: *spouse, parent, sibling,* and in many homes, more specifically the gendered version of each of these. Many of us auto-execute the characteristics of these imprinted role definitions as soon as we enter those roles as adults. Even if our professed desire is to *do the role differently* than the example seared into our brain, we still end up behaving almost exactly the way we observed others behave when we were young. Sometimes we are aware we are doing this; sometimes we are not.

This is often most obvious when people become parents. They swear they will *never* act the way their mother or father did, but as soon as their child is born, or as soon as their child gets to a certain age, they begin to treat their child the way their parent treated them. This behavior isn't limited to parents. Romantic partners do the same thing. A woman will promise herself she'll never make herself responsible for her partner's happiness in the same way her mother constantly *made nice no matter what* so as not to upset her father, but as soon as she and her partner become legally married, she finds herself acting just like her mom. Or maybe a man truly wants to have an equal relationship and doesn't expect his partner to give up their dreams to support his, but as soon as they move in together he begins to act just like his dad did and assume his life goals *naturally* come first.

It takes intentionality to change this auto-behavior, and you have to notice and admit this knee-jerk response is happening before you can get intentional about changing it. It's especially difficult to notice you're behaving exactly the way you promised yourself you wouldn't if the *story* you tell yourself and others is about how you'd never be willing to act that way. You're not lying to yourself. You mean every word. You really do want to behave differently than your mom did as a wife, or than your dad did as a husband. If you had two moms or two dads, this is all still true. You still witnessed how each spouse behaved and were still imprinted with two specific types of roles in romantic relationships. If you were lucky enough to have good role models, that can help. But things are further complicated by the huge pile of expectations our culture and social groups dumped on top of the role definitions imprinted on our young absorbent brains. Most of us absorbed many over-the-top perfect picture expectations of how love should be, along with various unhealthy, predetermined, and gender-specific *duties* and *entitlements*.

All of these predetermined influences can be difficult for us to notice because they often dwell in our subconscious. This means we start acting in ways that conform to these role definitions seemingly without thinking. But, it's not that we aren't thinking, it's that we aren't aware of our thinking because it's happening subconsciously at lightening speed. It's a lot like having your response on speed dial. Once something within our given role – wife, husband, whatever – triggers our predetermined role definition, it's as if we start mechanically acting from a memorized script.

Not only are we *pre-wired* as children and

acculturated by society and our subgroups to act in specific ways in our relationship roles, we also are the product of the particular love language and currency we experienced while growing up. Some of the ways we behave in our relationships are influenced by how our family:

- defined the word love
- defined loyalty
- expressed affection
- communicated with each other

Once again, because assimilating our family's *system* of love happened at least partially at a subconscious level, we are not always aware of applying this same system to our current relationships. We may sometimes find ourselves extremely annoyed at our partner when the situation doesn't seem to warrant it, but nonetheless we can't seem to stop feeling so upset. This may be because our partner has done something that demonstrates they are not using our familiar system of love. This may invite us to believe they don't truly love us. *Wouldn't they use the expected system to demonstrate their love if they actually did love us?* we ask ourselves subconsciously. Meanwhile, we aren't completely aware of having this thought; we are only aware of a deep sense of disquiet, of feeling as if our partner did something *wrong* that wasn't *enough*.

When this happens, your partner is probably going through a similar smorgasbord of feelings. Each of you may be unaware of *why* you are feeling what you're feeling. You try to have conversations about what's going on but since you aren't completely in touch with your own feelings, what you're talking about is often *not* what you're talking about.

So, first things first – we need to recognize our definition of love and our expectations for our role and our partner's role in the relationship. This includes getting in touch with our version of each of these, based on how we've been pre-wired through our family's modeling, and preconditioned by societal influences large and small. We then have to choose how we want our current version of each of these things to be. It helps to pay attention to what we have said to ourselves and to others about these things. It also helps to notice the reactions we have when we watch how other people act and expect others to act in their relationships. Some of our responses may be based on our prewiring and preconditioning but others will undoubtedly give us insight into how we aspire to be in our relationships.

It is important to note that this process isn't about villainizing our family's habits or choices. Rather, it is about learning from what we were shown and choosing what we want to emulate, what we want to edit, and what we want to reject completely. Sometimes negative examples are really good teachers.

Then we need to *notice* how we are functioning in our relationship and determine if our actions fit our desires. If they don't, we can begin to tweak them until they get closer to the way we want things to be. This process will undoubtedly produce *this-feels-better moments,* but often it will also feel uncomfortable. It will include times where we find ourselves returning to our auto-settings and becoming discouraged. And that's not the only difficult part. Along with being willing to tell ourselves the truth about all of this, we also need to communicate openly and honestly with our partner.

Our partner may be thrilled about our intended journey or may become threatened by it. They may or may not grasp the concept of automatic emotional muscle memories that have to be unlearned in order to begin to behave in new ways. They may want to join in and attend to their own auto-settings. If you choose to begin to examine your auto-settings, you may discover your partner is too scared to look at their own tendencies and expectations and doesn't want to stick around while you explore yours. That sounds like a risk, but is it? Why would you want to stay with someone who wants you to hide who you are, and who you aspire to be, to make them feel more comfortable?

It would be amazing and wonderful if you and your partner had the same definition of love, currency of love, and role expectations. It could happen, but often it doesn't. But as long as those things are complementary, and nothing either of you expects clashes with what the other person expects, you can still be together in a good way, if you are clear about what you expect. This works even better if you both communicate in a manner that helps each of you to *create* what you want, instead of to *hide* from or *attack* what you fear.

It *is* possible for two people to love each other deeply and not have complementary expectations about relationship roles. It is also possible to have compatible expectations even though the relationship doesn't end up working out well. It takes a certain amount of bravery to be honest with your partner about what you expect in your relationship, especially if you are hyper-focused on trying to avoid disapproval or the possibility of a break-up. You have to believe, or at the very least choose to begin to believe, that you deserve to be loved. And not just to be loved, but to be loved for who you are.

Remember: Be brave enough to be seen so you can be loved for who you really are.

CHAPTER 3
Blinders

Imagine a woman you know, telling you the following story: *I ran into my ex unexpectedly when I was shopping in town. He acted like a total jerk and was as self-centered as ever. One minute he tried to impress me by bragging about things I don't particularly value but that he thinks make him a big deal. The next minute he used a phony sounding voice to dish out digs-disguised-as-compliments, pointing out what he sees as my inferior attributes and circumstances to try and make himself feel superior. Listening to his shtick was exhausting. I made an excuse to get away from him as quickly as I could without causing a scene or bursting a blood vessel – mine or his!*

Imagine the woman then goes on to tell you what happened when she shared the gory details of her encounter with her ex. Several of her friends responded by asking: *What did you expect? Aren't those behaviors some of the same ones that made you decide to leave him?* When she told her friends she was surprised to discover that she hadn't expected her ex to act that way, they asked her, *Why not? Did you think he would start acting differently or would stop doing the things that bothered you, just because you left him?* She agreed with her friends that her ex's behavior shouldn't have surprised her. Why do you think it did?

Since she probably hadn't come in direct contact with his unpleasant behaviors since they had broken up, she may have activated the classic: *out of sight, out of mind* response to being separated from her ex's behaviors. But maybe she also told herself: *If I don't see his bad behavior, it doesn't exist.* This would have been somewhat of a developmental regression on her part. Babies don't develop *object permanence* until they are around 8- or 9-months old. Before they acquire this ability, they perceive an object as being *gone* – not just *out of sight* – when it is covered up with something such as a blanket or a pillow. This is why babies enjoy the game of *peekaboo* so much. They are repeatedly surprised and delighted when an object magically *returns*.

It's as if the woman was acting as if her ex's behaviors – the ones her friends had so helpfully reminded her were part of the reason she had chosen to leave him – no longer existed. She bought into this distortion of reality because she wanted to believe she would never have to encounter his obnoxious behaviors again. In a throwback to an earlier developmental stage, the woman lost sight of the fact that *unseen* doesn't equal *gone*. She had chosen to believe her ex's behaviors no longer existed *because* she couldn't see them. Perhaps the woman didn't realize she had been viewing things this way until she was surprised by her ex's behavior when she ran into him.

This *if I don't see it, it doesn't exist* response isn't just limited to break-ups. It can also happen in a current relationship. We metaphorically close our eyes or look away from behaviors we wish our significant other didn't engage in, and we pretend those behaviors don't exist. We may do this diligently and intentionally, or we may only subconsciously realize we are doing it. If and when other people point out our significant other's undesirable behaviors, we tell these people they are mistaken. We swear these behaviors aren't happening. We aren't aware we are lying to them because we aren't aware we are lying to ourselves. Sometimes we apply this *if I can't see it, it isn't there* response to our own behaviors too. We look away from what we are doing and pretend it isn't happening.

When we finally experience these behaviors – ours or someone else's – in a situation too disturbing to ignore, it is suddenly much more difficult to continue denying the truth. We become devastated when we are forced to face the truth. The now-seen behavior itself is upsetting, but at a deeper level, more of our pain comes from the fact that the false world we created for ourselves – a world removed from our significant other's (or our) unpleasant behaviors, and all they may imply – has come crashing down around us. We are forced to face our fears about what these negative behaviors may indicate: *What if my significant other doesn't care about me, or respect me, as much as I think or hope they do? What if I'm actually not that nice of a person?* We created our alternate reality to protect us from discovering the answers to these questions.

We think utilizing this type of *looking away* protection keeps worst-case scenarios away, but instead it keeps us in the dark and prevents us from discovering the truth about our situation.

Remember: Many choose the dark when they fear what the light will reveal.

CHAPTER 4
Miracle Growth

CHAPTER 4

Imagine you are in a relationship and one of the small things you want your partner to do, although you don't consider this a deal breaker, is to go dancing with you. You really enjoy dancing, but your partner always says, *I'm just not feeling it,* whenever you suggest it. You have plenty of friends you could go dancing with, but you want to do it with your partner. Dancing for you is about more than the music and the steps. To you, it is an amazing way to connect with the person you love – locking gazes, the rhythmic movements the two dancers mirror and answer, and the teasing touch-and-retreat of bodily contact.

It isn't as if your partner dislikes dancing. You met them at their cousin's wedding. They were in the bridal party, so they did quite a bit of dancing. And they were good – really good. Their reluctance to go dancing with you obviously isn't based on a lack of confidence. They also are always totally willing to attend loud, crowded shows when their favorite bands are in town. They don't do any dancing at these shows but they aren't claustrophobic or put off by the noise.

They say they don't understand why *not* going dancing with you is such a big deal. You don't think you're asking too much. You're not looking for a regular Saturday night dancing date; you just want to go once in a while. They figure you should be willing

to go with your friends who enjoy dancing as much
as you do. You try to explain that going with your
friends isn't the same. Your partner doesn't get it.
Your requests continue to be met with the same *I'm
just not feeling it* response.

First you feel sad and a little hurt – *why won't
your partner do this little thing for you? It really isn't
a lot to ask.* You worry their unwillingness is a sign
they don't love you as much as they say they do.
This thought frightens you, so you become angry.
You complain. You badger. You give your partner
every opportunity to change their mind, to prove
how much they care by acquiescing to your request.
They tell you that you are the unreasonable one,
that you are blowing things way out of proportion.
*It's just dancing – what difference does it make
who you dance with?* They tell you it makes more
sense for you to go dancing with other people
who also really enjoy it. They accuse you of
being *oversensitive* and *unreasonable*. They pat
themselves on the back for not being jealous about
you going out with other people.

Eventually you realize your partner is never going
to budge. You become resigned to going dancing
with your friends. You have fun when you go, but
your partner's absence always diminishes the

experience for you. You become resentful. You simmer. You stew. You never completely forgive your partner for being unwilling to go dancing with you, but you decide to stop bugging them about it because you are afraid further discussions might reveal how little they care about you. You bury this worry somewhere deep inside and ignore it.

Over time, other incompatibilities arise in your relationship. You discover you each have very different ideas about how you want to be in the world, and about how you want to be in your relationship. The two of you decide to break up. It's mostly a friendly split. There is no shouting, no name-calling, and no voiced accusations. You both agree it would be a mistake to stay together. Because of this, you are surprised when you start crying over the loss of the idyllic relationship you had hoped for when you first met your partner. Your brain knows this *picture perfect* relationship would never have been possible with this particular partner, but your heart hasn't caught up yet.

Fast forward several months – you hear your partner has met someone new. You're happy for them. This is partially possible because you've also met someone else, someone you really enjoy being with, AND they like going dancing as much as you do. Besides, you learned a thing or two from your last relationship. You have a better idea of what's important to you, of what you want.

One night when you and your new partner are out having an amazing time dancing, you suddenly catch sight of your old partner dancing with their new love interest. Your stomach drops. You feel horrible. You feel betrayed. You don't notice that the things you love most about dancing – the rhythmic physicality of touch and the soulful eye contact aren't happening for you and your partner, because your focus is elsewhere.

You feel cheated by the fact that your old partner is obviously willing to go out dancing with someone else. You convince yourself this means they must love this new person more than they loved you. You wonder why your old partner pretended to care so much about you when it is now obvious they never did. Your mood goes from sad to furious as you realize your old partner just totally wrecked your evening.

The thing is – *you're* actually the one who ruined your evening.

Remember: Your partner's behavior is a reflection of who they are, not a reflection of who you are.

CHAPTER 5
Former Faces

Sometimes when we're in a relationship, the other person doesn't truly see who we are because they are projecting someone from their past onto us. It's as if we are wearing a mask that looks like their disapproving parent, or as if we are walking around inside an avatar that resembles their former lover who treated them in reprehensible ways. Our partner usually doesn't realize they are *seeing* us in these ways. Imagine one partner says: I *love that shirt on you*, and the other partner hears: I *want to be the one who decides how you dress*. That's not what their partner said; it's also not what they meant, not even in the slightest way. But that is what was *heard*.

Why does this happen? Someone may become over-sensitized to certain words or even to specific areas of their lives, such as what they choose to wear, because of a traumatic or extremely negative experience they've had in the past. They also may have subconsciously-set, auto-responses to particular behaviors they encounter because of something negative that repeatedly happened to them in the past. They installed these auto-responses in order to make sure they will never again have to experience what happened in the past. Their defensive response may be to attack their partner head-on, to collapse in misery and dejection, to smother their partner in *understanding*, or to distance themselves emotionally from their partner. Any way they choose to react – no matter how irrational or confusing – is their attempt to avoid or deflect what they fear is beginning to happen in the relationship.

This fear invites them to become hyperaware of anything their partner does that even vaguely reminds them of an undesirable past event. They often instantly overreact without taking the time to discover what is actually going on. They wouldn't mind knowing the reality of their current situation if it's good, but they may subconsciously decide it would be better not to know, just in case their current partner turns out to be as big of a jerk as the last jerk. Under this avoidance is their true avoidance, which probably looks something like this: *Why do all my partners seem to be jerks who treat me poorly? Will I ever be able to find anyone who will treat me well? Is there something wrong with me that I don't know about?* They are hopeful things will be different this time, but there's very little likelihood they'll be able to build a positive relationship with their current partner if they keep seeing some past jerk superimposed over their partner's face.

Many of us get caught in a cycle of relationships similar to this situation. We continue to judge our current partner through a fog of distrust and mistaken identity. We keep repeating the same types of relationship experiences without learning what we need to learn. This pattern can last much longer than it needs to if we aren't aware of *why* we're doing what we're doing in our relationship and why our partner is doing what they are doing. Reflecting on what went wrong in our not-so-fabulous encounters can help us to learn about what we do in relationships. We can also begin to more clearly define our relationship must-haves and deal breakers.

If our partner freaks out and acts as if we are being controlling when we suggest somewhere we'd like to go to dinner, and we respond by criticizing their behavior without investigating what's behind it, things usually deteriorate quickly. This is apt to be even more likely if we happen to be oversensitive to being unjustly accused. If this were the case, your partner would assume you were acting like a controlling jerk, and you would assume they were being a judgmental jerk. You each would be reacting to negative experiences you carried forward from the past, instead of responding to what was actually happening in the present moment. Both of you would probably have convinced yourselves of the need to root out these unwanted behaviors, at the tiniest hint of the possibility of their existence, or end up destined to spend the rest of your life enduring them. But what if you are misreading what is happening in the present because you have been traumatized by past events?

If either partner assumes things are as *they have been in the past* – and no discovery happens to confirm or disprove these assumptions – then escalation, mistrust, and jerkitude will undoubtedly reign. The partners' joint fears feed off of each other and create a tumultuous and dangerous whirlwind of emotion that fosters mistrust and resentment. It becomes difficult to truly get to know each other when all you see is *what you fear you'll see.*

Choose to pause before you overreact. Choose to pause before you react at all. Figure out what you each are talking about. Acknowledge and communicate your fears to each other, but instead of walking around on eggshells and demanding that your partner take care of your feelings, be responsible for your own feelings. Decide to discover what is actually happening in a particular situation; then determine if it is similar to or different from what you fear. Use your intellect, your life knowledge, your intuition, and perhaps your instincts – instead of your fear – to explore what's happening. Then respond to what is happening and *just* to what is happening, not to what has happened in past relationships of whatever kind.

You cannot force your partner to look at their fears. They have to choose to do it. You can suggest. You can model. You cannot control their behavior. Do not try, because that would simply be another form of jerkitude. Even if your partner *does* want to uncover their fears, their actions may take longer to catch up to their intentions. They may be hampered by their continued belief that their worst fears will eventually come true, and revert to their auto-responses from time to time.

Focus on your own discovery process as you explore your fears, your intentions, and your behaviors. Choose to step away from your own jerkitude. This makes it easier to notice when others are operating based on fear and not seeing you for who you really are.

Remember: Sometimes we all allow nightmares to keep us from seeing what's real.

CHAPTER 6
Self Centric

When I was in grade school I would ask my mother if my friend, Claudia could sleep over. My mom would answer the same way every time: *If Claudia wants to sleep over, she needs to get her mom to bring her here and to pick her up when she's ready to go home.* Claudia would talk to her mom and make it happen. A week or two later when I would ask my mom if I could sleep over at Claudia's house, she would say, *If Claudia wants you to sleep over at her house, then her mom needs to come and get you and bring you back.* I'm sure you can see how self-serving my mother's responses were. It was even obvious to Claudia and me at the time. What was also obvious was that there was no way around my mother. We were powerless to change her. If Claudia and I wanted to sleep over at each other's houses we had to convince her mom to do the driving.

This type of behavior sometimes shows up in relationships in less blatant ways. But, more often, it increases in frequency and intensity over time. No matter how subtle or extreme these behaviors may be, they are all a version of an *accept-or-reject* response. This response is present when one person in a relationship expects, insists, and ultimately demands that something has to be done their way no matter how the other person feels about it.

Imagine you and your partner have agreed not to have any beef in the house. You partner eats beef, but you don't. You also really don't want beef to be cooked in the house, because it grosses you out to see it raw. Your partner readily agreed to your no beef request. It appeared to be a kind and friendly concession on their part. However, now your partner always assumes the two of you will go to their favorite restaurant, the Steak House whenever you go out to eat. This expectation has never been voiced or agreed to; your partner simply makes reservations at the Steak House, without consulting you, anytime the two of you plan on going out to eat.

Here's the problem: there isn't much for you to eat at the Steak House. They have a choice of baked or mashed potatoes, decent but not great bread, and a so-so but not horrible salad. You can eat those things, but they don't comprise a good meal or even a nutritious one. You'd like to enjoy a special meal when the two of you do get to go out. You don't go out to eat very often as a couple. You go out even less often with friends. You don't mind going to the Steak House once in a while since it is your partner's favorite place. They could get steak somewhere else, but they don't want steak somewhere else. They like the steak at the Steak House the best, so that's where they want to go. They don't seem to notice your lackluster meal – they are too busy enjoying their steak.

You feel as if there is an unacknowledged form of revenge taking place. In-between the lines, you think you hear what you suspect your partner isn't saying out loud: *If you won't let me have beef at home then you can't have a nice meal when we go out.* You tell yourself you are imagining this. You try several times to make your partner understand you would like the two of you to go to a different restaurant at least once in a while, a restaurant where you would both enjoy your meal. Your partner always reminds you that the steak at the Steak House is the best in town and that's why they want to go there. You are invited to feel selfish for trying to take this away from them, *especially since* you already took beef away from them at home. They intimate that they are the better, more considerate partner in the relationship because they were willing to concede to your needs even though you won't do the same for them.

Some part of you realizes this isn't true. Your partner seems to have no problem not eating beef at home and in fact really looks forward to and enjoys all the meals you make. They also take pride in making fantastic pizza and spicy good stir-fries for the two of you. Newsflash: your partner is gaslighting you. They are inviting you to believe their version of reality is true even though it is a lie. You are invited to believe it would be completely selfish of you to begrudge your partner their Steak House dinner. You are also invited to question your read on what's happening. It's as if your partner is telling you that you can't trust yourself to know what's true.

Did you see what just happened? The partner who selfishly wants everything to benefit them – the one who is willing to invite you to feel out of touch with reality, to feel like a bad partner – has manipulated their recounting of the situation to make it appear as if *you* are the one being selfish. This is one version of the accept-or-reject response. This partner is saying: *Accept what I want, exactly the way I want it, OR you will be rejecting me.* Anything you are not willing to do your partner's way, no matter how minor, is seen as a treasonous act and as a rejection of your partner rather than as a rejection of what your partner is asking you to do.

Another example of this would be if your partner started to tell you that one of your good friends isn't someone you should trust. This friend happens to be the one you can talk with about anything, and they never judge you. When you assure your partner that your friend has always been trustworthy, they tell you that you aren't seeing things clearly. Your partner begins to twist small things your friend says and does in an attempt to convince you to reconsider and accept their *don't trust them advice*. You are thrown off guard. You become frustrated. You get irritated. Your partner tells you they're only trying to protect you. They tell you they are looking at your friend more objectively than you are. You choose not to buy into what your partner is saying. They continue to disapprove of your friend. They show this disapproval in subtle verbal and nonverbal ways whenever you spend time with, or talk to your friend. Your partner always wraps their disapproval up in their self-proclaimed honorable intention of protecting you. Your partner begins to portray your continued relationship with your friend as a rejection of your partner's wisdom and of their desire to protect you. Eventually you are invited to view continuing your relationship with your friend as being disloyal to your partner. You feel as if you have to choose. You know if you choose your friend, you will lose your partner. Once again, you have been invited to accept your partner's views or to be treated as if you are *rejecting* your partner.

It doesn't matter whether what you partner wants, or more accurately demands, from you is something as small as insisting you always put all the mail in a pile face-up, or as large as turning your back on someone you care about – their behavior is always the same. They insist you wholeheartedly comply with their expectations or else they will treat you as if you are rejecting *them*. If you reject your partner, they will punish you: they will reject you in turn, either by distancing themselves and threatening to leave, or by acting as if they are the victim of your horrible treatment of them.

A partner who uses the *accept-or-reject* response isn't interested in hearing what you have to say; they don't want your opinion. They want you to prove you care about them by blindly doing whatever they ask of you. This may be because they are insecure and fear you'll leave them. They may feel they need to constantly test you to reassure themselves that they love you. The bottom line is, you are not allowed to disagree with them. Failure to completely and immediately agree with whatever they want, no matter how big or how small, will always be seen as you rejecting them.

This kind of behavior isn't healthy. It's also sneaky. It plays on the roles we've been conditioned to fill and the relationship definitions and expectations we've been fed. If we focus on trying to keep the peace or on compromising for the *good of the relationship,* we may end up never allowing ourselves to have an opinion. Becoming responsible for your partner's emotional well being – never disagreeing with them or questioning them in any way – is no way to build a healthy relationship. Neither is demanding that your partner do this for you.

Remember: You shouldn't be expected to give up you when *you* become an *us.*

CHAPTER 7
Boundaries

Most people think of boundaries as lines they tell other people not to cross. Sometimes we literally don't want them to enter into our physical space. The *Keep Out* sign on an older sibling's door discourages a younger sibling from crossing into forbidden territory. Sometimes we deliver a *cease and desist order* via a spoken boundary: *You better not be thinking about mouthing off and disrespecting me right now.* Sometimes a raised eyebrow can be a silent *step away from that line before you make yourself sorry you crossed it* boundary. All of these boundaries attempt to control someone else's behavior.

What if we looked at boundaries a different way? What if boundaries were about *our* behavior rather than about *other people's* behaviors? What if we used them to indicate what we were choosing not to be a part of, not to engage in? What if we acknowledged that trying to control someone else maybe isn't something we actually *should* be trying to do?

This sounds frightening. How will we be able to keep the monsters out if we don't draw boundaries to stop them from coming in? Let's picture a boundary drawn to keep the monsters out. Can you see it? The monsters are where they belong on the *other side* of the boundary. We are on this side of the boundary, on the *safe* side. We may be smiling because we know the monsters aren't on our side, or we may be shaking our fists at them and yelling things such as: *That's right, you stay over there! You're not allowed to cross this line!* Whether we're grinning in triumph or shouting in anger, we are still facing the monsters. The monsters are still having an impact on our lives. We are still actively engaged in a relationship with the very monsters we are trying to avoid.

What if we changed three things about the boundaries we draw?

Let's start with the boundary's purpose. Imagine a boundary. It's on the ground just in front of you. Someone who is doing something inappropriate is on the other side of the boundary. Instead of saying something to them such as: *Don't you be bringing that nasty behavior over here,* you say: *I choose not to engage in that stinky behavior with you. I'm done with it.* The purpose of this boundary would be to indicate where you won't go rather than to mark where you forbid the other person to go. You are controlling your own behavior instead of attempting to control someone else's behavior.

Next, let's consider a new position in relation to the boundary we've drawn. After you draw your line and communicate your message, turn your back to the boundary. This is different than the sentry-like stance we are used to seeing. The guards at Buckingham Palace face toward us, not away from us. They are protecting by staying vigilant, by never taking their eyes off potential threats. Choosing to turn away — to literally turn your back — demonstrates your decision to disengage from whomever or whatever is on the other side of the boundary you just drew. This is more than a physical separation — it is a demonstration of your intention to emotionally disconnect from the negative drama associated with an undesired behavior. You are sending a clear message to the person on the other side of the boundary and to yourself: *I will no longer participate in this behavior in any way. I am removing my attention, and I am choosing not to give any heart or brain space to this behavior. I will reflect on what happened but only to learn more about myself.*

Finally, let's look at what we do after we've drawn the boundary and turned away from it. In a perfect world, you would flow off toward better things carrying forward whatever you had learned from this negative situation. But real life is rarely like this. What often comes next is an invitation to feel as if you've been too harsh or too lenient. You may feel guilty because you understand *why* the other person did what they did. You may feel compassion for them. This means you are a caring person. But don't be a sap. Choose to be unwilling to be treated poorly by someone even when you understand their story and care about them. This makes you a strong person. You may start to dream of revenge or feel as if the other person needs to be punished for what they've done to you. This means you are human. It's also usually a waste of time. People rarely truly change because we punish them. Google the studies if you don't believe me. Besides, this is simply another version of you trying to control their behaviors or emotions. It's better to use all that passion to create the life you want by focusing on your own behaviors and emotions, and continuing to explore what makes you tick and grow.

If you're completely honest with yourself when you reflect on what happened before you drew your boundary, you may discover how you contributed to the situation. This doesn't change the need for a boundary. It doesn't negate the other person's part in the scenario. It does provide a good chance to learn more about yourself. You may feel the need to apologize. There's nothing wrong with that; however, make sure you apologize *only* to communicate what you've realized about your contribution to what happened. Do not convince yourself that your apology means the other person isn't responsible for what they have done. Do not allow your need to apologize to open a door in your boundary wall, unless that is your well-thought-out intention. Instead do some version of writing a message on a paper airplane and sending it over the wall. Then turn your back again. If you are only apologizing to get forgiveness or to give the other person an opportunity to apologize to you as well, don't bother. This is merely another way of attempting to control the other person's behavior. Step back. Don't cross that line.

You should also make sure your boundary line isn't actually a wall of anger. There's nothing wrong with being angry but check to make sure you aren't using your anger as a defense against discovering how you contributed to what happened. Also notice if you are *still* in a relationship with the other person, only now one based on anger rather than love or friendship. If your heart and brain are often filled with their presence then they are still very much a part of your life.

Boundaries don't have to be terminal. They can also be drawn within healthy relationships. For example, if you were to say to your partner: *I will not engage in a conversation with you when you start to belittle me. It doesn't matter if you call it teasing. I choose to separate myself from this behavior of yours. I will not take part.* You wouldn't be telling the other person to stop; you would be communicating your choice to stop being part of the conversation. You would not be attempting to control their behavior but rather your own. If it happened again, your message might look more like this: *I told you, I am not willing to engage in a conversation with you when you start to belittle me. It doesn't matter if you call it teasing. I choose to separate myself from this behavior of yours. I will not take part. I know you think this is a little thing, but it is a big deal for me. This is not how I want to be treated.*

Whenever you draw a boundary like this within an ongoing relationship you need to figure out if the behavior is something you are willing to continue to repeatedly step away from, or if it is a deal breaker for you. Don't stay quiet about your feelings and then up and leave without ever telling your partner that something was a deal breaker. Be honest with yourself and with your partner.

Remember: Your boundaries should be about your behaviors not someone else's.

CHAPTER 8
Do-overs

When we hold onto leftover anger from a prior relationship and use it to direct our current choices, we are often also still holding onto the prior relationship itself. We may be attempting to *do over* the past in the present in an attempt to replace or to overwrite a former, disastrous relationship with a better one. Or maybe, we are less interested in getting it *right* this time and more interested in proving we were the *wronged* party in our past relationship. *It wasn't our fault. We were misjudged. We were taken advantage of. We were mistreated. We didn't have a chance.* We need to believe, true or not, that our ex-partner was an idiot, a creep, or maybe even a monster.

We don't want anything that remotely looks, sounds, or even smells like our old relationship. Perhaps, because of this, we may choose to be with someone we can easily control. Maybe we are drawn to someone who doesn't bother to get close enough to truly see us, let alone to judge us, because they are so extremely self-obsessed. But if we choose someone we can control we may become bored; or worse, we might begin to behave in some of the same ways as our loathsome former partner. If we felt like an accessory, a meal ticket, or an interchangeable presence to keep loneliness away in a former relationship, we may now choose to be with someone who puts us on a pedestal. This plan is likely to backfire, leaving us confused when we begin to feel suffocated by the weight of our partner's unending attention, and surprised that we also feel isolated and alone.

These kinds of choices are made to avoid re-experiencing an unpleasant behavior from the past. We are intimately familiar with the symptoms of the behavior we want to avoid, and like a good poker player we can recognize even the smallest telltale signs of its presence. We are so hyper-focused on avoiding what we don't want, we put almost no energy into creating the kind of relationship we actually do want. Knowing what we don't want is helpful, but it's not enough. Staying fearfully focused on the past to avoid repeating history often keeps us stuck in our history instead of allowing us to learn from what has happened. We need to shift our focus from what we are trying to avoid to what we want to create. Ask yourself: *What can I choose to say and do that will allow my partner to see who I really am and to feel comfortable enough to show me who they really are?* Neither of you should have to hide how you feel or pretend to be different than you actually are.

It's vital to let your partner know what is important to you in a relationship. But first you have to figure

out what *is* important to you. There are some things
we each feel are nonnegotiable in a relationship.
Often when we compromise on these things we end
up turning into a quivering mess or acting like an
angry maniac. Of course, there are some people who
react this way when their partner doesn't want the
same paint color for the walls as they do. We're not
talking about that; we're talking about core values.
We're also not referring to the many choices in life
that are simply about preference. Core values are
the things we feel we must have to be true to who
we are. Maybe you don't want to be lied to, not just
because it's unpleasant, but because at your core you
are unwilling to live a life based on anything other
than truth. You meet someone wonderful who says
they'll never lie to you about anything important. You
don't understand why you feel furious and devastated
when your partner lies about little things that don't
matter to you. You are confused. Your subconscious
isn't. It understands what is going on. The lying *does*
bother you. It doesn't matter that the lies are about
little, unimportant things. You are compromising and
being untrue to one of your core values. You cannot
build a relationship with someone else when you are
attacking yourself.

There is an *important* distinction here: you are the
one compromising your values; your partner isn't

doing it. Your partner is simply living life based on their values, AND their values are different than yours. Your two sets of values are incompatible if one set of values creates a climate that makes it next to impossible for the other set to flourish. But your values don't have to be exactly the same. They can be complementary instead – blending together the way different notes do to create a beautiful harmony. But remember – your core values are absolutes. They cannot be partially implemented. You are either living according to your core values or you are not.

Do our core values change over time? Maybe. If they do, I'm guessing it's a rare occurrence, but that's not what matters. What matters is what your values and your partner's values are *right now*. And a word of advice: let go of trying to change your partner's core values. If you find yourself wanting your partner to be different, to change fundamental things about themselves, what you're probably saying is that you want them to be someone else. They can't be someone else. If you want someone else – leave and go find them. Seriously. Don't try to remold your partner into who you want them to be. Either decide to choose to stay with them for who they are or recognize that the relationship isn't working. This is another kind of do-over – when you want to give your partner an emotional makeover so they become who you want them to be. Sometimes we don't want to give up the good part of something even when another of its parts isn't good for us. We can get away with occasionally choosing to eat foods we crave that make us feel sick, but a steady diet of those foods wouldn't be a good idea. We don't want our relationship to require us to continuously manage debilitating emotional intolerances or reactions either.

There are numerous ways to compromise that have nothing to do with our core values. These compromises provide opportunities for us to demonstrate our willingness to create an environment that works for everyone in the relationship. But it is insulting to expect anyone to be someone other than who they are.

Even if you don't realize that's what you're doing, your partner probably will. Your behavior may invite them to feel as if they aren't *enough* for you or as if there is something *wrong* with them. Maybe they are a really cool human but they simply don't see the world the same way you do. Maybe what's most important to you is something they barely notice, or something they see in a radically different way. If a puzzle piece appears as if it's going to fit but it's not the right piece, you can't force it to fit, no matter how hard you try.

Remember: Get over trying to *do over* the past or to *make over* your partner.

CHAPTER 9
Clone Sightings

We humans have a tendency to see others through the lens of our own experiences. For example, we may become overly eager to label our friend's relationship as a bad one if it seems at all similar to something unpleasant we experienced in a relationship. We may be even more likely to do this if we still blame our former partner for what went wrong. Choosing to believe that most relationships turn ugly may help us to continue to hold onto our version of reality – the one in which we see ourselves as the victim. We suddenly start *seeing* bad relationships everywhere, because the more unhappy relationships we notice, the less responsible we feel for our part in the demise of our former relationship. It's as if we are Oprah saying, *You get a crappy relationship, and you get a crappy relationship, and you get a crappy relationship* to everyone we meet.

If we feel a friend is being taken advantage of the same way we were, we may begin to see them as a victim. Because of this, we may fail to notice our friend's contributions to the disharmony and misunderstandings in their relationship. We are more likely to be blind to their contributory behaviors if those behaviors in any way resemble choices we ourselves have made. These choices may be ones we are not yet willing to acknowledge, let alone take responsibility for. If our friend's partner does anything

remotely resembling what our partner did, we may
rush to villainize them and to advise our friend to be
careful. We invite our friend to doubt their partner's
trustworthiness. If their relationship is flourishing
even though it appears to be similar in some ways
to our disastrous one, this dissonance isn't likely to
sit well with us. We *need* to believe our friend is
overlooking something potentially devastating in
their relationship. We don't believe we were at fault
for the way our relationship crashed and burned,
but we aren't willing to risk finding out that we were.
It feels safer to continue to blame our ex-partner
and to avoid exploring any other reason for our
relationship's failure.

We don't notice the relationship advice we give
to our friends isn't necessarily helpful, because we
believe we are protecting them from future harm
only we can see. But our subconscious goal may be
less about saving our friends from pain and more
about confirming our own story. But our story may
be more of a cover-up than a tell-all, especially if
we fear we caused our former relationship to fail or
that there is something that keeps other people from
loving us. To avoid thinking about these fears, we
label everyone as either a victim or a villain, and
reassure ourselves we must be the victim, because
we have never acted like a despicable villain.

We would swear it wasn't true if anyone accused us of giving inaccurate advice to our friends in order to make ourselves feel better. In reality, we aren't sharing what we've learned from our previous relationships because we haven't learned anything from them. We can't learn from our experiences because we are too afraid of what we will *uncover* if we explore what happened to us. *What if we did contribute to what went wrong? What if we never figure out how to get the love thing right?* These fears invite us to commiserate about our bad experiences with others to reassure ourselves things didn't work out for us solely because our partner turned out to be a jerk.

Or maybe, one of our friends thinks our current partner is a jerk. Our friend tells us not to trust our partner. Their advice doesn't make sense to us. It doesn't feel right. We know our friend cares about us and means well, but frankly, they seem a little too intense about what's going on in *our* life. If we are too scared to confront and refute our friend's assessment of our relationship, we may start to believe them and unintentionally begin to morph *our* story into their story. We *can* refuse to allow fear to convince us some trumped up worst-case scenario is suddenly true. We can choose to bravely and authentically consider what our friend has said to us. It wouldn't be the end of the world if we discovered something that has the potential to become a problem unless it gets a little maintenance. We can decide to keep the parts of our friend's advice that fit and reject the parts that don't.

What happens when we, or someone we know, is caught in this loop of needing to brand everyone else's relationship as a failure in order to avoid exploring what happened in their own relationship? How do we get off this Mobius strip of avoidance and accusation? It really helps if you can figure out what you are working so hard to avoid thinking about. Once you know what that is, take a deep breath and disengage from the terror of what you think you might discover if you think about whatever you are trying to avoid thinking about. If something is wrong in your relationship, it would be better to know about it sooner than later. And if you discover things are as good as you thought, well then, now you aren't just hoping or assuming things are good, you actually *know* they are.

Use what you observe your friends saying and doing in their relationships to help you learn about what *you* do in your relationship, rather than as ammunition to judge what's going on in their lives. Realize you can't *make* your friends learn about themselves or about their lives. They have to choose to do that for themselves. Remember your friends' experiences aren't necessarily the same as experiences you have had. In fact, the experiences *you* are having right now may not be exactly like the ones you've had before. This doesn't mean you can't still be learning or perfecting the same life lessons you were working on in the past even though you are now at a different time and place in your life.

It is also important to understand that everyone who isn't very nice isn't necessarily a monster. More importantly, everyone who reminds you of someone you used to know isn't automatically exactly the same as that other person. Instantaneously labeling people as victims or villains doesn't protect you – it just oversimplifies things so you don't have to learn more about yourself. Here's the thing: learning about yourself is the ONLY way you can improve your life and your relationships. Other people's behaviors don't define who you are. Your response to those behaviors does. If you stop blindly trusting or blaming others, you can start seeing them more clearly. You can also start taking responsibility for your own behaviors. If you discover someone is a jerk-stuck-on-repeat, you can choose to walk away. If someone turns out to be a monster, you can get yourself the hell out of there, even if you need to get help to make that happen. If you decide someone is a keeper, and they decide the same thing about you, you can nestle in and create something good together.

No matter how things turn out, you can choose to learn about yourself – about what you need, want, give, request, do, and hesitate to do. The more you know about yourself, the more of yourself you can share. The more you share, the more vulnerable you are. The more vulnerable you are, the more open you are. The more open you are, the more you can be filled with all the good things. And yes, if you're open, you also risk being offered undesirable things. But if you *are* open, you will be aware, and you will SEE those undesirable things for what they are. You will say *no thank you* because you will know you get to choose to accept or reject what is offered. Anytime and all the time.

Remember: If you want to sort out your life, stop labeling things without discovering what they really are.

CHAPTER 10
Love Not War

They say *all is fair in love and war*, but too often we end up confusing love with war. We put on different types of armor – to protect ourselves from disappointment, from disillusionment, from rejection, from pain of any kind. We are strategic in our maneuvers. Our tactics are designed to protect the perimeters of territories we remember losing in former skirmishes. We are hyper-alert. We see danger over every rise. We trust almost no one. We are ever-ready to do battle if we must.

But, love is *not* war. And yet, it often *is* difficult to ignore the survival techniques that have been drilled into us. We would feel less-than-responsible if we abandoned our prime directives. We would feel powerless without our armor, and we don't see any benefit to being vulnerable and exposed. Everyone knows being *seen* makes you weak. You can't let the enemy get to you. If the enemy does attack, we must cease to think of them as someone we care about if we want to survive. We must show no mercy. We must protect ourselves. Our hearts may hope for everlasting joy and happiness, but down in the trenches of everyday life, we choose to focus on walking out of each encounter unharmed.

Love should not be something we have to fight to survive. It also shouldn't be indentured servitude. And, it's not a fairytale, no matter what anyone told you or promised you. Love, of whatever kind, in any type of relationship, is about safety, comfort, support, and respect – in both directions – to and from each of the people in the relationship.

- *Safety* means you are seen and accepted for who you truly are, and for who you aspire to be.

- *Comfort* means you are free to make mistakes without being judged or ridiculed.

- *Support* means you are valued, and encouraged to strive to be the best version of yourself you can be, rather than being humored for choosing so-called unrealistic ambitions or force-marched toward goals someone else wants to impose upon you.

- *Respect* means you are expected to know your own mind and to make your own choices – choices that may or may not be the ones your significant other would choose for themselves.

In an ideal relationship, each of us would always treat the other in these ways, AND each of us would also treat ourselves in these ways. But ideals are what we strive for, not necessarily what we currently have or need to achieve to be happy. It's not about obtaining our chosen ideal – it's about agreeing to journey together *toward* it. It's about choosing to support one another whenever we misstep individually or collectively. It's about agreeing to always tell each other, and ourselves, the truth, no matter how glorious or frightening the truth may be.

Remember: A relationship without truth is merely a business arrangement.

ABOUT THE AUTHOR

Cinse Bonino is a former professor of Creativity &
Conceptual Development with a background in
Education and the Psychology of Human Learning.
Cinse does one-on-one awareness sessions (in person
and online) to help individuals better define and create
the way they want to be in the world. She also presents
and leads workshops on: creativity, problem solving,
communication, teaching and learning, and personal
awareness. Cinse is the author of *The Ride of Your Life:
choosing what drives you* and the creator of *Wise
Asks* cards. Cinse lives in Burlington, Vermont, with her
cats Jasper and Melina, and enjoys widely spaced but
deeply appreciated visits from her son who currently
serves in the U. S. Army.

Check out Cinse's offerings at: seechoosedo.com

Special thanks to:

Lindsey Rae for her ability to spot missing commas and sentences devoid of clarity

My seemingly evil grandmother – secretly one of my best teachers

Everyone who has ever asked for advice and caused me to create metaphors to help them

Cover art & design and book layout by the fabulously talented Mollie Coons molliecoons.com

www.ingramcontent.com/pod-product-compliance
Lightning Source LLC
Chambersburg PA
CBHW051036030426
42336CB00015B/2898